Annual Report

FOR THE YEAR ENDED DECEMBER 31, 1955

ILLINOIS CENTRAL RAILROAD
Main Line of Mid-America

Illinois Central:
Main Line of Mid-America

By Donald J. Heimburger

With photographers Jerry Carson and Owen Leander

*All-color photography of the largest
north-south railroad in the United States*

Jerry Carson

Dedication
To Amy and Alison.
Dad will probably find a train.

Acknowledgements

In a sense, I've been working on this book since I grew up alongside the Illinois Central tracks at Tolono, Illinois in the 1950s. It was there I saw my first IC trains, and that's where my IC journey began. Along the way, I've met many IC fans and historians, and to them I owe a great deal of thanks for their cooperation in putting this book together. I would especially like to thank Jack Bailey, Henry Bender Jr., Jerry Carson, Rich Gajnak, Owen Leander, Phil Mikalauskas, Bob Nicholson, Russ Porter, Brad Smith, Dick Stair, the late Clayton Tanner, Dick Wallin, Philip Weibler and Charles Zeiler.

Library of Congress Catalog Card Number: 94-74490
ISBN: 0-911581-35-9
First Edition
Printed in Hong Kong

HEIMBURGER HOUSE PUBLISHING COMPANY
7236 West Madison Street
Forest Park, Illinois 60130

Contents

Foreword

Locomotive #2429, a large 4-8-2, pulls its six-car green passenger train consist south out of Chicago and past Soldier Field (at right). IC's Central Station at 12th Street is at left of train in background. *Glass plate photo, collection of Rich Gajnak*

With so much rich history behind it, the Illinois Central, the main north-south railroad in the United States, has taken on a prestigious image. Many great men have played a part in the development of the Illinois Central through the years—Abraham Lincoln, Stephen A. Douglas, Henry Clay, Daniel Webster, Stuyvesant Fish, John Jacob Astor, Edward H. Harriman, Andrew Carnegie and William Averell Harriman.

The railroad is a result of the leasing or merging of more than 200 railway companies, the oldest of which was the West Feliciana Railroad in Mississippi and Louisiana. By the time the Civil War began, the IC was operating nearly 1,700 miles of track. No other railroad played more of a role in the establishment of the great central region known as Mid-America than did the IC.

The IC could not operate without dedicated people to run it, and the thousands of IC employees through the years have shared a vision of just how great the railroad had been and could be in the future. A family atmosphere also permeated the conciousness of employees for a very long time.

DEDICATION TO DUTY

When I went out on field trips during my years as a member of the IC Public Relations Department, I noticed a dedication to duty unlike I had seen in other industries. The dispatchers, station agents, brakemen, shopmen, superintendents, porters, conductors and cooks were all serious about their jobs, and many gave a good portion of their lives to working for the IC. Having so many people working for so long at one job made the IC seem more like family to employees. They came to work with the knowledge that other people just like them were coming to work too, for a great railroad, a railroad with a proud past. Their common bond was the IC, a place where life-long friendships developed.

4

This book is my tribute to a gracious railroad, a line that operated the famous streamlined *Panama Limited* in first class style beginning in 1942. An experience never forgotten was eating the King's Dinner, which included a cocktail, appetizers, fresh Gulf shrimp cocktail, wine, fish, charcoal broiled sirloin steak, potato and vegetable, salad, dinner bread, coffee, cheese and apples, coffee and liqueur—all for $9.85.

INDUSTRIOUS RAILROAD

This book is my tribute to an industrious railroad, a line that opened the first shaft coal mines in southern Illinois in 1855 and that shipped the first fruit under refrigeration in 1866 and used debris from the Chicago fire of 1871 as fill for IC trackage to enter the City of Chicago.

This book is also my tribute to an enterprising railroad, a line that began the first institutional advertising program that was unique in the railroad world. The program, launched in 1920, ran for more than 30 years, appearing in nearly 500 on-line newspapers. It was intended to bring the public into the IC's confidence. And it worked.

The IC was the first land-grant railroad, a pioneer in crop diversification, re-forestation, one of the first commuter railroads to convert to electric operation and was a leading proponent of unit gain and coal trains.

It was also one of the railroads to continue to improve passenger train service. As late as 1967, a new passenger department was created and placed under the direction of the railroad's first passenger vice president. A new all-reserved-seat

The 100 year medallion and map were common markers in 1951 when the railroad celebrated its centennial. *Jerry Carson*

A 2-8-2 Mikado #1775 with a short perishable train sits at the lakefront in Chicago; the train carries white flags. The IC was the first to ship fruit under refrigeration in 1866. *Glass plate photo, collection of Rich Gajnak*

The Illinois Central moved a large quantity of perishables, including bananas unloaded from ships in the Gulf of Mexico, and transported them to Chicago at the foot of the Great Lakes. *Don Heimburger collection*

coach train was introduced that year between Chicago and New Orleans. Amtrak took over just a short 3½ years later.

FIRST MAJOR EMPLOYER

I knew the IC as my first major employer after college. When I joined in 1969, many new things were afoot at the railroad including advanced computers, adding the new Woodcrest repair shop south of Chicago, a heightened demand for piggyback service and unit trains, new double-deck commuter cars, diversification, a merger with the Gulf, Mobile & Ohio, and enactment of the Rail Passenger Service Act which led to Amtrak.

My service for the company now seems short, just a quick few years where I was part of a family of down-to-earth railroad people, who always made sure the railroad and its future came first. The staff was benevolent, smart and innovative. The job was probably one of the best ever formulated for a railfan—writing railroad stories, taking railroad pictures and riding railroad trains.

In earlier years I grew up watching IC's heavy coal drags with Mikados zipping down the main line at Tolono, Illinois. The pictures in my mind of IC steam power remind me of O. Winston Link's 1950s night time scenes he captured on the Norfolk & Western: these pictures are vivid, I saw IC steam mostly at night, and it was in the 1950s.

ON A SCHEDULE

The world was a simpler place in the 1950s, and all that mattered was being able to watch the IC's long freight trains, and especially the streamlined passenger trains, thunder through town, cutting their path southbound to New Orleans *on a schedule.*

Diesel locomotive #4001, an E-6A built in 1941, and a Central of Georgia 2,250-hp EMD E-8A built in 1950, sit in Chicago in the fall of 1958. The IC and CofG pooled equipment for Florida-bound travelers. *Jack Bailey, Don Heimburger collection*

Watching their orange, chocolate brown and yellow-striped passenger cars and locomotives *race* through the crossover at Tolono was a sight that impressed even the only-curious railfan.

On a warm summer evening, the agent would step outside the station to catch a breath of fresh farm-like air and breathe in the aroma of prairie weeds, as well. The distant rumbling of the approaching passenger train sounded ominous. The steel on steel rumble quickly gathered momentum and became deafening, and the whistle blowing for the two crossings in town was virtually continuous. As the diesels approached the Wabash diamond, the engineer cut out the motors, restarting them again once past the diamond. The trains sped past the depot in 100 mph territory (roller-bearing equipped cars and passenger locomotives were allowed 100 mph between Champaign and Branch Junction, Illinois, a distance of 122.2 miles). The silence of the diesels' whine was only momentary, and the re-start noise, plus the heavy streamlined cars hitting the diamond one after another, added a tumultuous roar.

CAPTURES PRAIRIE MILES

At that speed, the sound lasted only a few seconds, as the streamliner captured prairie miles faster than the wind. The train's fading sound, however, lingered for several minutes, then became less, and finally faded into the sound of friendly crickets alongside the track near the station. This sight—and the sounds—played out several times each day at Tolono, as well as hundreds of other towns along the IC line.

The time has passed for these events, but the pictures are still there in my memory; in fact, the IC of old is still there. The

freight trains, some with Mikados on the lead, still manage to pull their loads across the rich, black Illinois flatlands and eventually down through the Mississippi swamps. The people—yes, the IC people—still go to their jobs every day, toiling to make the railroad a better place.

The passing of the years seems to sharpen the memory in some respects, and this book is a tribute to all those men and women who worked for the IC, or who were ever associated with the IC in any way, and those who rode the IC as passengers or just watched from afar as the trains rolled by. I hope you enjoy this trip back into the past. After all, besides our memories, it's about all we really have left of the old, proud Illinois Central Railroad—Main Line of Mid-America.

Donald J. Heimburger
August, 1995

A huge Mountain 4-8-2 #2548 with auxiliary tender prepares to move out of the yard servicing area to its train. Note the apparently new tender plates patched into the old. The IC Mountains were a hallmark of steam locomotive design. *Owen Leander*

The Illinois Central in 1951

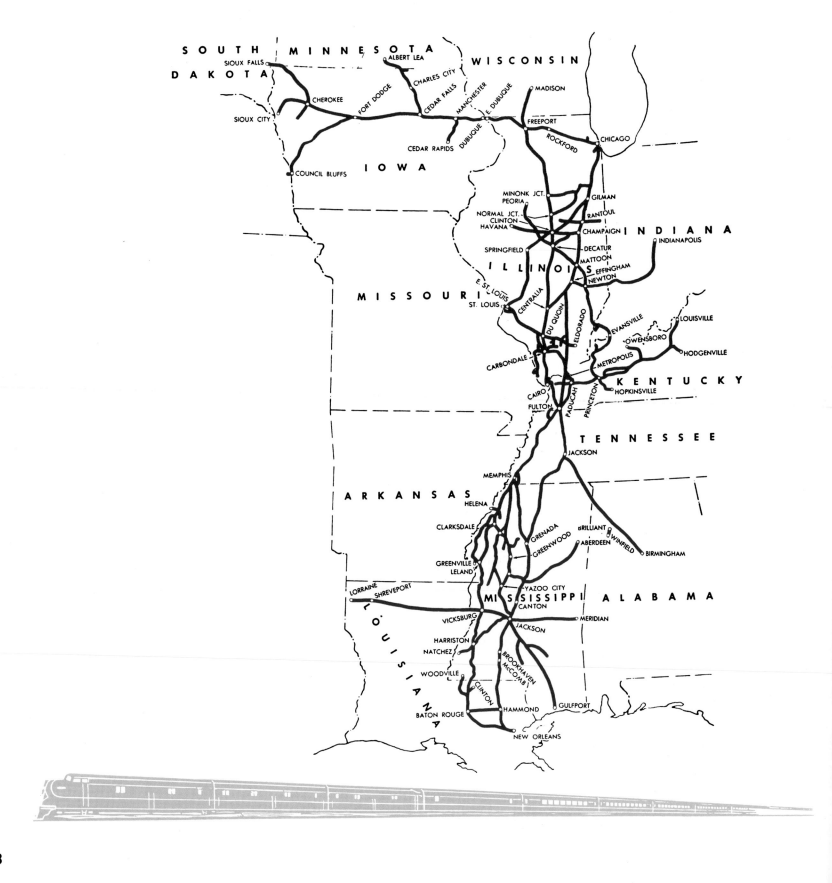

IC Steam: Giants of the Prairie

The Illinois Central Railroad owned many steam locomotives with common wheel arrangements, such as 0-8-0s, 2-8-0s, 2-8-2s, 2-8-4s, 2-10-2s and 4-8-2s. But it also owned some with rather odd wheel arrangements, such as the 0-8-2 and 0-10-0. One common type, the 4-6-4 Hudson, was an uncommon type on the IC, the road owning only one which was rebuilt from a Lima 2-8-4.

IC's locomotive classification system was largely defined by locomotive wheel arrangements and by number series. IC also rebuilt many of their own steam locomotives in the Paducah Shops, which did a superb job of providing the railroad with the steam power it needed. With low-cost on-line coal and an efficient supply of steam power provided by Paducah Shops, the IC was slow to dieselize.

Steam locomotives shown in this roster section beginning on page 29 are arranged primarily by wheel arrangement and by series numbers within that section, although there are some exceptions. **IC**

The first-ever excursion train operated by the IC was to Kankakee, Illinois on August 5, 1853 from Chicago. Kankakee was reached just a month earlier by track-laying gangs on July 11. Here one of the last active IC 0-8-0s, #3503, a Baldwin product originally constructed in 1921, sits sheltered in the Kankakee roundhouse in January of 1958. The locomotive was finally retired two years later in 1960, along with others of her class. *Russ Porter*

TOP. The year 1955 was good to the IC. The railroad bought a buffet luncheon that year for each shareholder who attended the annual meeting. This husky 4-8-2 Mountain pulls through Monee, Illinois with some of the cars that earned revenue that year. *Jerry Carson*

LEFT. Located in the southern Illinois coal fields on the Zeigler District, Herrin was a coal town. This November 1957 scene shows #1583 in the company of the black gold that kept IC's rails shiny. *Philip Weibler*

NEXT PAGE. The sky fills with thick, black smoke as #1462, a 2-8-2 tugs at its train of hoppers near Herrin in November of 1957. *Philip Weibler*

TOP. The rich Illinois prairie was long a site for IC steam. The iron horse helped transform the unproductive wilderness into a land of agricultural and industrial activity. Mattoon, Illinois didn't exist in April of 1855. By August there was a large hotel, post office, dry goods store and two groceries. Lima-built #1227 2-8-2 commands a train of merchandise rolling across that vast prairie. *Owen Leander*

LEFT. At the beginning of 1947, the Main Line of Mid-America owned twenty 4-8-2s of the 2600-2619 series, and a total of 136 4-8-2s, compared with 60 locomotives of the same class in 1936. Shown: IC #2611. *Owen Leander*

TOP. #2742 was one of a number of modernized 2-10-2s; it was built in 1923 and retired in December of 1959. The locomotive is shown at Paducah, Kentucky, to which track was laid around 1852 and at which a giant locomotive shop was constructed. *Jerry Carson*

Between 1850 and 1900, then 13-state-wide IC helped push the population fourfold, the value of farmland leaped by 13-fold and of manufactured products 28-fold. East of Irwin, Illinois in November of 1957, a 2000-series 4-6-2 helps expand the commerce in the region even more. *Russ Porter*

TOP. The IC was a business railroad: the 14-state IC territory produced 77% of corn grown in the U.S., 23% of wheat, 50% of cotton, 43% of cattle, 70% of hogs, 90% of iron ore and 33% of bituminous coal. This servicing scene was repeated time after time in IC land during steam days. Location: Carbondale, Illinois. Date: October, 1954. *Jerry Carson* RIGHT. The older Pullman green IC passenger cars were a source of warmth for travelers in the winter and cool comfort in the summer; IC brought air conditioned cars to the line in 1931, with a fully air conditioned train named the *Diamond Special* being placed in service in 1932. *Owen Leander* NEXT PAGE, BOTH PHOTOS. #2750 (top) and #2553 are both of the working-class variety of locomotive on the IC. The #2750 is a strapping big 2-10-2 and #2553 4-8-2 had been built from a 2-10-2 in 1942. *Owen Leander and Jerry Carson*

The IC reduced grades beginning in 1897 between Gilman and Springfield, Illinois from 58 feet to 26.4 feet per mile, thus increasing the tonnage ratings of locomotives by 88 percent. The #1391 is north of Gilman in the 1950s. *Jerry Carson*

Carbondale, a "true" IC town, hosts big 2-10-2 #2747. *Philip Weibler*

TOP. Half a year after this picture was taken, IC 2-8-2 #2121 was scrapped. Rebuilt from #1600 in 1941, it's putting in its time here at Carbondale in early 1956. *Jerry Carson*

Roaring down the line near Kankakee in November of 1955, Mountain-type 4-8-2 blasts steam and smoke into the chilly air and shakes the frozen ground. Kankakee was a good location to watch the IC's speeding locomotive giants. *Jerry Carson*

TOP. A 4-8-2 and 0-8-0 workhorse share facilities as they are renewed for further service at Centralia. Tonnage through Centralia increased so that by 1902 a parallel line was built to Cairo. *Richard Wallin*

LEFT. A large 2700 Class 2-10-2 #2742, with partial rust attacking its tremendous smokebox, and extra tender coupled for longer runs between servicing, signals off and departs the water tank at Paducah on July 24, 1957. *Jerry Carson*

NEXT PAGE, TOP. The year before this photo was taken, 1954, the IC was in the finest, most efficient operating condition of its long, distinguished history. Net income in 1954 was $22 million, and the road employed 34,500 people. The #2500 Class locomotive demonstrates the power the IC's mid-50s Mountains produced. *Jerry Carson*. BOTTOM. At Fulton, Kentucky, the IC branched out five routes; thus, steam was always on the ready here, as evidenced in this mid-50s power showing. *Jerry Carson*

TOP. IC tenders leaned toward the lengthy side, allowing longer runs over the Main Line of Mid-America with fewer stops for water and coal. The 1500s featured Walschaert valve gear and 63½" drivers. *Russ Porter*

RIGHT. In the late 1940s, the IC's 0-8-0s were numbered 3300 to the 3500s except four assigned to the Chicago & Illinois Western which carried the numbers 801-804. *Philip Weibler*

PRECEDING PAGE, TOP. Six and a half miles from Kankakee sits the little burg of Irwin, Illinois where in June of 1957 a vintage Nash and Ford frame a 900 Class 2-8-0 steam locomotive, way car and long freight on the Freeport to Cairo line. *Russ Porter* BOTTOM. Heading down the Clinton, Illinois line from Champaign at the wye near the tower, a 2100 Class 2-8-2 pulls its freight train west in the early 1950s. *Dick Stair*

The IC was capable of putting on a spectacular smoke and steam show at any time on its lengthy route between the Great Lakes and the Gulf of Mexico. In November of 1955 near Bradley, Illinois, #2527, a former Central-type 2-10-2 converted to a 4-8-2, alternately darkens and whitens the prairie air. *Jerry Carson*

IC #2817, a monster 2-10-2, checks out with a freight at Paducah on June 6, 1955—the year the railroad reached 379 diesel units systemwide. By May of that year, the Iowa, Vicksburg and Springfield divisions were completely dieselized. *Jerry Carson*

The rays of a cold February, 1955 sun reflect off a 4-8-2s shiny black boiler as it heads toward the Windy City at Homewood, Illinois. The IC's use of steam power in later years was based on the modernization of steam locomotives and the large supply of low-cost coal available near IC rails. *Jerry Carson*

A steam locomotive washdown wasn't exactly a rarity on the IC; like its passenger trains, the IC liked to put its best freight foot forward. Engine #2710, renumbered from #2961, a Lima product of June 1921, receives a cleansing bath from a caretaker in October of 1957 at Centralia, Illinois. The engine was dropped from the roster between 1960-1962. *Richard Wallin*

The abundant coal fields near Central City, Madisonville, Dawson Springs and Princeton, Kentucky kept IC trains loaded and moving. Between 1910 and 1930 on the railroad, the products of mines more than doubled, going from 11.2 million tons in 1910 to 25.9 million in 1930. *Philip Weibler*

General merchandise—and coal—is moving through Central City, Kentucky in August of 1957. A 4-8-2 and a 2-10-2 pull their trains past the Central City depot. *Philip Weibler*

A 4-8-2 Mountain is in charge of an IC mail train; during the Wayne Johnston years, passenger train deficits mounted, due in part to declining mail revenue. *Owen Leander*

NEXT PAGE. What would it be like to be in IC's Carbondale, Illinois in 1957? Locomotive #2747, a 2-10-2, is there amist the activity. *Philip Weibler*

A smokin' 2600 Class Mountain with a long freight train puts metal wheels to metal rails north of Mattoon, Illinois in July of 1953. Steam locomotives still roamed the IC in 1953 with 847 units versus 1,106 diesels, and the Main Line of Mid-America still operated 6,500 miles of main line track. *Jerry Carson*

Two Mountains, Nos. 2433 and 2441, come together at Fulton, Kentucky on a warm June day in 1955. The year before, more than one third of IC's freight train operations had been dieselized. These titans of the IC rails have limited time, too. *Jerry Carson*

The largest IC shop was located at Paducah and was reputed to be the most modern locomotive shop in the country in 1951. It covered 110 acres, 21 of which were under roof, employing 1,200 workmen. Here a Lima-built 2-10-2 tugs its hopper load around Paducah. *Jerry Carson*

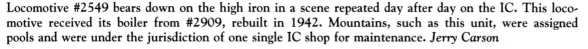

IC was known for its hotshot freight trains. Here #2611, a Paducah-built 4-8-2 with large 70" drivers, pulls a merchandise and coal train through Illinois prairie sometime in the 1950s; the engine was retired in 1960. *Jerry Carson*

Locomotive #2549 bears down on the high iron in a scene repeated day after day on the IC. This locomotive received its boiler from #2909, rebuilt in 1942. Mountains, such as this unit, were assigned pools and were under the jurisdiction of one single IC shop for maintenance. *Jerry Carson*

Fast approaching the south Chicago suburban town of Richton Park, Illinois, this #2500 Class engine with auxiliary tender plys some of IC's heaviest rail, where traffic is also heaviest. *Jerry Carson*

Stationed and ready at Central City, Kentucky, 1500 and 1600 Class 2-8-2 steamers huddle in June of 1954 until their next assignment. *Jerry Carson*

The air is heavy with the smell of steam, smoke and lubricating oil at the Champaign, Illinois roundhouse in the fall of 1956, a time of transition on the railroad, new improvements and more technological advances. Steam is beginning to end its career on this mighty north-south railroad, and these 0-8-0s and 2-8-2s lodged at Champaign will be turned to scrap. *Philip Weibler*

A quartet of 1500 and 1600 Class Mikados bask in the fading light, perhaps an omen of the ending days of IC steampowered machines. As early as 1951, the road was one of the last Class I lines using steam for all of its over-the-road freight hauling. *Philip Weibler*

Steam Locomotives

2-2-4T

Rogers-built 1880 2-4-4T Suburban-type was still around at Markham, Illinois when this photo was taken in October of 1957. It was used in Chicago IC commuter service. *Jerry Carson*

0-6-0

Fifty-one-inch drivered Alco 0-6-0 sits at Champaign, Illinois yard in August of 1955. By then, the IC's steam switching fleet was a little more than 100 units. *Jerry Carson*

2-6-0

IC #401 2-6-0 is a Brooks locomotive built in 1888 and retired in 1916. *Owen Leander*

2-8-0

Built in 1918, #329 was sold by the IC in 1953 to the Paper Calmenson & Co. A number of the IC's 0-6-0 and 0-8-0 switchers were sold to mining, sand or gravel companies. *Owen Leander*

Rogers provided a number of 2-8-0s to the IC in 1903, including #733, which featured 57½" drivers and tractive effort of 32,243 pounds. *Jerry Carson*

Rogers-built 2-8-0 #740 was originally numbered #709 and scrapped in 1954. *Owen Leander*

RIGHT. One of many IC locomotives to retire to a scrap line, waiting perhaps to see if it would be later recalled for active service, #909 was eventually sold after 22 years of IC service. *Jerry Carson*

4-6-2

BELOW, LEFT. Handsome 4-6-2 #1137 awaits a highball as the sun highlights its stark white numbering and lettering against its black superstructure. *Owen Leander*
BELOW, RIGHT. At Carbondale, #1155 on January 1, 1956. *Jerry Carson*

Perhaps #1177 was recently outshopped, for it appears it has just been repainted in IC black and sent back to the motive power fleet for more duty. *Owen Leander*

2-8-2

Built in 1915 by Lima, #1225 2-8-2 was renumbered from #1727 in 1944 and renumbered again in 1954. Three years later it was gone from the roster. *Owen Leander*

IC's Bloomington District was originally the Kankakee & Southwestern which ran from Otto, Illinois to Normal 80 miles away. A wye at Otto connected the Chicago District tracks with the Bloomington District tracks. The junction was controlled by an interlocking tower. Locomotive #1457 is at Otto in July of 1955 with a freight. *Jerry Carson*

Locomotive #1462, a 2-8-2, at Carbondale in November of 1957, presents a fine picture of IC steam. *Philip Weibler*

The 1500 Class of 2-8-2s was numbered from 1501 to 1599 (also 1600) and included Baldwin-built locomotives constructed between October, 1912 and May, 1914. A number of these were later converted to 0-8-2s and 2-10-0s. They were nearly all gone by August of 1957, and finally scrapped, retired or dropped from the roster by 1960. The 2-8-2s on the IC helped to haul much of the tonnage and were used extensively except for very high speed or very heavy grade conditions. *Owen Leander*

Locomotive #1536 releases thick black smoke as the engineer complete with traditional coveralls, white gloves and red bandana, heads towards the cab. *Owen Leander*

Mikado #1545 (originally #1738) is a Lima-built locomotive that was retired in February of 1960. *Owen Leander*

IC #1587 steams at Bluford, Illinois on May 25, 1955. Bluford was located on the Edgewood Cutoff, a 169-mile supplementary line from Edgewood, Illinois to Fulton, Kentucky. Work was begun on the cutoff in 1925 to ease the growing traffic on the main line trackage; Fulton was the "center" of north-south traffic. *Henry Bender Jr.*

At Carbondale's roundhouse, 2-8-2 #1680 slumbers in July of 1956. *Jerry Carson*

At Fulton, on a warm day in June of 1955, Mikado #1594 looks recently out-shopped. At Fulton, three IC Kentucky lines were linked together. *Jerry Carson*

IC's pretty Pacifics included #2034, rebuilt during World War II. *Jerry Carson*

IC 4-6-2 #2065 sits at Central City, Kentucky as the spring of 1960 approaches and a rapid depletion of the steam locomotive occurs. In January, 1960, 219 steamers remained on the IC roster, but only 43 as of December 31 of that year. In 1960 the IC still operated about 10,500 miles of total trackage. *Jerry Carson*

The 2-8-2s were the workhorse of the Illinois Central: #2120 had 64½" drivers and 225 pounds of boiler pressure. It was scrapped in May of 1955. *Owen Leander*

IC #2125 was a 2-8-2 rebuilt from #1642 in January of 1942. It was scrapped in 1956. *Owen Leander*

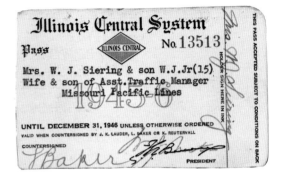

IC #2128 was allowed to serve the IC until December of 1959, two and a half years after this picture was taken at Paducah. In 1959 coal continued to be IC's largest source of revenue, actually dropping 2% in 1959 by 50,000 tons. *Jerry Carson*

Of the same class as above, 2-8-2 #2132 had 30 x 32" cylinders and lasted until 1955. This old machine could tell a number of interesting stories if it could talk. *Owen Leander*

Date: July 25, 1957. Location: Paducah. Class: 2100s, 2-8-2. A black Geep sits behind; by the beginning of 1959, the IC already owned 387 general purpose diesel locomotives. *Jerry Carson*

4-8-2

Handsome and huge, with attached auxiliary tender, 4-8-2 Mountain #2405 features 73½" drivers and 58,389 pounds of tractive effort. The 2400s, built by Alco and Lima between 1923 and 1926, remained until February of 1960 when the last was retired. *Owen Leander*

IC's 2500 Class 4-8-2s consisted of numbers 2500 through 2555, all built with other locomotive boilers between 1937 and 1942. #2502 was retired in 1959. *Owen Leander*

At Paducah in July of 1957, IC #2507 is stately and strong, and two years away from being retired. *Jerry Carson*

ABOVE. Hugging the rails, #2517 pulls its merchandise load south of the Windy City environs. *Owen Leander*

Seventy-inch drivers make the 4-8-2s look impressive. *Owen Leander*

ABOVE. Mountain #2530 and extra tender sit at Paducah in 1957. *Jerry Carson*

Running the freight this day on the race track south of Chicago is #2531. *Owen Leander*

PREVIOUS PAGE, TOP. Mountain type #2523 and others converge, but #2523 looks sharp after an apparent outshopping. BOTTOM. #2528 prepares for a highball. *Both photos, Owen Leander*

ABOVE. IC #2539 smokes it up in the yard. *Owen Leander*

While a railroad construction gang prepares a new spur to the right, a large 2-10-2 roars around a banked curve in this glass plate photograph from the collection of Rich Gajnak.

ABOVE. Three IC work-horses pictured include #2714, a 2-10-2, #1425, a 2-8-2 and another unidentified locomotive. The photo was taken at Benton, Illinois on the 52-mile line between DuQuoin and Eldorado, originally the Belleville & Eldorado Railroad.
Jerry Carson

IC #2736, a 1921 Lima-built 2-10-2, simmers along-side a sister locomotive.
Owen Leander

LEFT. Catching its supply of fuel, water and sand before heading out onto the main at Paducah, #2739 and auxiliary tender ply the facilities tracks in July of 1957. In that year, IC employed 31,352 people. *Jerry Carson*

The fireman and engineer crowd the window as #2750 waits in the yard with its train for a highball. *Owen Leander*

Recently outshopped, #2803 at Freeport, Illinois was built by Lima in 1921 and rebuilt with a new boiler by IC's Paducah Shops. She was used with other locomotives of her class on the Iowa Division's Dubuque District in meat train service. *Owen Leander*

5839. Illinois Central Depot, Champaign, Ill.

IC #1536, a 1914 Baldwin 2-8-2 with 63½" drivers, and #2805, a bigger brother 2-10-2 from Lima in 1921 (renumbered in August, 1944 from #2942), wait on parallel ready tracks to lead their next trains. *Owen Leander*

Formerly #3013, IC #2807 sits at Paducah a day before July 4, 1958. *Jerry Carson*

Lima-built #2812 is three years away from being retired in 1960. Paducah, July 25, 1957. *Jerry Carson*

IC #2817, a 2-10-2, appears to be newly out-shopped at Central City, Kentucky on June 9, 1954. Even the bell received a coat of black paint. *Jerry Carson*

0-10-0

IC #3601 is an 0-10-0 switcher acquired from the Atlanta & Vicksburg in 1926; it was scrapped in 1955. *Owen Leander*

An 0-8-0 is at Carbondale, Illinois on January 1, 1956 a year from scrapping, having been built in 1922. *Jerry Carson*

0-8-0

BELOW. #3509 0-8-0 occupies the scrap track at the Champaign roundhouse in June of 1961. *Clayton Tanner*

With a pleasing black paint covering her boiler, cab and tender, #3513 goes about her duties on the IC system. *Owen Leander*

ABOVE. Freshly painted coal hoppers at Centralia get a pull from #3544 on May 3, 1955. *Henry Bender Jr.* RIGHT. #3566 and another IC locomotive combine efforts on a string of freight cars. *Owen Leander*

2-10-0

This class, rebuilt from 2-8-2 boilers and 2-10-2 chassis, were numbered #3610-3624 between 1939-1941. *Jerry Carson*

ABOVE. #3624 was built from a chassis and boiler from other locomotives; the clean locomotive sits next to one of IC's many black water tanks. *Owen Leander*

The #3621 gets a check of its boiler front; the engineer looks on and is ready to give his locomotive some throttle. *Owen Leander*

51

Prior to World War II, the IC upgraded much of its equipment and rebuilt a number of 2-8-2s into an unusual wheel arrangement, an 0-8-2. *Owen Leander*

NEXT PAGE, TOP. The #3787 had 63" drivers and 185 pounds of pressure. BOTTOM. IC 2-8-2 #3969 was acquired in 1926 with the Alabama & Vicksburg and Vicksburg, Shreveport & Pacific purchases. *Both photos, Owen Leander*

Another 0-8-2 was #3691, shown here under steam sometime in the 1950s. In 1959, the IC was still growing. It merged with the Alabama & Vicksburg and the Vicksburg, Shreveport & Pacific Railway. It also purchased the Tremont & Gulf Railway and acquired three miles of the Canton & Carthage and constructed 14 miles of line known as the Corinth and Counce in Tennessee and Mississippi. *Owen Leander*

In 1942, the IC converted 83 locomotives to other classes and steam pressure was increased on 188 locomotives. At right is IC #3697, an 0-8-2. *Owen Leander*

ABOVE. This Chicago exposition featured classic railroad equipment, including this IC 2-8-4 Mountain built by Lima in November of 1926. Large offset brass bell and old red and white IC logo on the overhead feedwater heater makes the locomotive distinctive. *Rich Gajnak collection*

2-8-4

Lima #8019 pushes its coal and covered hopper train at Reevesville, Illinois, 33 miles southeast of Marion. *Henry Bender Jr.*

ABOVE. Again at Reevesville, #8019 comes barreling through southbound with 26 cars on May 23, 1955. This is classic steam railroading in Southern Illinois on the Main Line of Mid-America! *Henry Bender Jr.*

IC #8020 survived nearly 30 years on IC property, finally being scrapped in 1955. *Owen Leander*

IC's Steam Finale

ABOVE. #1211, a 2-8-2 and #2726, a 2-10-2 were part of the great Illinois Central steam finale, a long line of rusting machines that were stored until the railroad was assured they were no longer needed: then they were disposed. These two were at Paducah on July 24, 1957. *Jerry Carson*

In line for disposition, IC's proud iron horses await their fate in Chicago freight yards on September 24, 1955. *Jerry Carson*

Flanked by fading power, a new IC two-bay hopper reveals itself in the background. Photo taken at Markham Yard, Illinois on July 10, 1955. *Jerry Carson*

Paducah was a holding location for soon-to-be-scrapped steam locomotives: here 2-8-2 #1600 rests its final days in the summer of 1957. *Jerry Carson*

The tracks next to the 85-foot-long turntable at Carbondale acted as holding tracks in 1958 for stored steamers. Nos. 1406, 2102, 2747 and 1589 occupy space there in the summer of that year. *Jerry Carson*

On the Property

Chicago

IC's million-dollar station on Michigan Avenue in Chicago was a beautiful structure, originally constructed in 1893 to help accommodate Chicago's World Fair traffic; it also housed the line's general headquarters. The large 10,000-light sign atop the structure was installed on August 19, 1948, said to be the largest and most elaborate west of New York's Times Square. *Russ Porter*

Built at the southern edge of Grant Park, Central Station, as it was called, featured a giant clock and tower which could be seen from the north Michigan Avenue area. *Russ Porter*

The south end of the station was constantly humming with trains and train workers. Here the *City of Miami* gets ready to depart at 8:30 a.m. in January of 1972. *Russ Porter*

ABOVE. In 1951, IC's board approved a sale of air rights on 3.3 acres of property to the Prudential Insurance Co. for $2.2 million. A 41-story $40 million office skyscraper was built there. *Russ Porter*

TOP, RIGHT. Chicago's skyline looking north from Central Station; IC's suburban electric trackage is at right. *Jerry Carson* The last run of the *SouthWind* (left) leaves Central Station; at right is IC's *City of New Orleans. Don Heimburger collection* IC's first piggyback cars were introduced in June of 1955; by the mid-1960s, the line was operating 171 flatcars for the service. *Russ Porter*

St. Louis
With the St. Louis arch in the background, an IC freight with varied power prowls the route. *Jerry Carson*

A good mix of IC steam occupies the Paducah roundhouse on July 25, 1957 including 4-8-2s, 2-10-2s, 2-8-2s and 0-8-0s. Already that winter, the Paducah Shops overhauled its last steam locomotive in that facility, #2741, a 2-10-2. *Jerry Carson*

IC #2741 is two years and two months away from being overhauled at Paducah Shops (see caption above). Here it is servicing the heavy IC coal traffic. *Jerry Carson*

Paducah

Galena

Clinton

Dubuque

IC #9502, a 2,000 hp GP-38AC with dynamic brakes pulls into Clinton, Illinois in 1973. *Russ Porter*

Crossing the wide Mississippi River westbound into Dubuque, Iowa is this IC freight with a typical 28-foot steel cupola caboose. *Russ Porter*

It's 1956, and more than 50 major railroads in the U.S. owned no steam locomotives, whereas the IC's comparable figure was 54 percent. Only 3 percent of passenger service was pulled by IC steam, however. The IC laid track to Galena in 1854, but the line was initially opposed by riverboat backers. Today Galena is an historic town that is reminiscent of turn of the century. *Russ Porter*

Central City

A rebuilt GP-9, #8199—and other diesels—idle at Kentucky's Central City engine facilities in summer of 1983. *Jerry Carson*

The IC owned more than 600 Mikados, ranking third behind the New York Central and the B&O. The #1518 is the sole survivor of the more than 600 Mikados owned by the IC; this locomotive is preserved in Paducah, Kentucky. *Jerry Carson*

Kankakee

The last 2-8-0 assigned to the Illinois Division in 1957 was #908, found here in the roundhouse at Kankakee. *Russ Porter*

A 2,400-hp E-9 with four EMD type D37 traction motors with an IC split-rail on the nose gets ready to depart at Kankakee in spring of 1971. Kankakee, milepost 55.9 from Chicago, was a major station stop for passenger trains. A four-track, six-arch concrete bridge spanned the Kankakee River south of the IC station. *Russ Porter*

With a Kankakee city bus on the overpass, IC Mikado #2134, one of 28 similar 2-8-2s built by Lima with 64½" drivers, passes through Kankakee on Oct. 10, 1954. Note caboose directly behind locomotive. *Jerry Carson*

Centralia

ABOVE. On Thanksgiving Day, 1958, at Centralia, Illinois, 4-8-2 #2550 is turned on the 100-foot-long turntable. That year the Centralia Shops constructed 177 new 50-ton steel box cars, and 50 new cabooses were built. *Dick Wallin*

In 1955, #2523 was one of 774 steam locomotives owned by the IC. It's handling a fast dispatch train at Centralia, but 1956 will bring a wholesale change of steam engines to diesels to handle through freight between Centralia and Chicago. *Jerry Carson*

NEXT PAGE. At Centralia in November of 1957 is #2608, among a group of twenty 70"-drivered Mountains built by the IC shops during 1942-1943. *Philip Weibler*

Gilman

Rounding the wye that ties into the main line in June, 1971 at Gilman, Illinois is #4034 from Illinois' state capitol, Springfield. It's heading up the *Green Diamond*, which featured the Palm Grove cafe car during IC's passenger years, but now operated by Amtrak. *Russ Porter*

An electic mix of a soiled 3,000-hp GP-40 #3022, a bright rebuilt GP-9 #8058 and some leased D&RGW F units arrive at Gilman. *Russ Porter*

Flossmoor

ABOVE. Passenger revenues increased in 1955 over the year before, bucking a national trend. A July, 1955 *City of New Orleans* speeds through Flossmoor, Illinois. *Jerry Carson*

ABOVE. The #4036, a 2,400-hp E-9, brings the *Panama Limited* into Flossmoor on July 23, 1955. Improvement in passenger business for 1955 reflected IC's superior service and the popularity of name trains. *Jerry Carson* RIGHT. In 1873, IC ferried its passenger trains across the Ohio River via the *H.S. McComb* which could carry six passenger cars. In this June, 1954 scene, the *City of New Orleans* crosses on the nearly mile-long Ohio River bridge and its approaches. *Jerry Carson*

Ohio River Bridge

Diesel Freights

A typical scene at Chicago in the late '60s was black and white (green diamond) Geeps and numerous dark green electrics. A year after this photograph was taken (1969), Penn Central, Lehigh Valley and Boston & Maine bankruptcies left IC with $1.3 million in unpaid accounts. *Russ Porter*

LEFT. On the "Gruber Line" at Tonica, Illinois, a twin pack of diesels switch the siding. A mile and a half north, a two-mile-long passing siding with 162 cars ran along the east side of the right-of-way. *Bob Nicholson*

ABOVE. Approaching Champaign-Urbana is the last special strawberry train the IC ran in 1959. The trains consisted of Railway Express refrigerator cars and a caboose. *Dick Stair* RIGHT. In early days, the IC laid temporary track across the Mississippi River over the ice; a train passes at East Dubuque, Illinois in June, 1970. *Russ Porter*

ABOVE. Used in the 1967 IC Industries annual report, this scene accompanied a Brainfare advertisement in regard to IC's "rent-a-train." *Collection of Don Heimburger*

LEFT. A trio of GP-38s pulling a freight pass underneath Burlington Northern tracks in East St. Louis, Illinois in December, 1972. *Jerry Carson*

Two 1,750-hp GP-9s lead an orange and white Geep through suburban electric territory in south Chicago in May of 1969. *Collection of Don Heimburger*

A pair of split-rail Geeps whine into the night as they perform switching duties for the Main Line of Mid-America. Unit #9389 is an EMD GP-9 with 1,750 hp and tractive effort of 44,600 lbs. *Jerry Carson*

A freight comes into Chicago's downtown area from its IC's Western Lines with packing house products, lumber, grain and perishables. The Chicago Board of Trade Building stands tall at the upper right; Central Station is to the right out of picture. *Russ Porter*

A freight emerges from the tunnel at East Dubuque, Illinois in December, 1967. In April, 1971 the *Hawkeye*, trains #11 and #12 between Chicago and Sioux City, passed through this tunnel for the final time. *Russ Porter*

The now-demolished station at Tolono, Illinois in the 1950s was an exceptional place to watch both IC steam-powered coal drags and Wabash time freights; this crossover saw numerous freight and passenger trains each day. *Clayton Tanner*

A 1967 scene near Elgin, Illinois honors the sturdy black and white Geeps of the IC; a green signal gives the go-ahead. *Russ Porter*

Commuters on IC's south suburban Chicago lines could witness up close the on-going roar of freight as the main line ribbons of steel paralleled the electric train tracks. *Collection of Don Heimburger*

IC personnel paralleled the Prairie State population in many ways: both were hard-working, devoted to their labors and dependable. This 1973 view of IC and neighbors tells a story repeated all up and down the line: the IC was "one of the folks." *Russ Porter*

By 1961, the IC had authority to operate over-the-road trucks paralleling 5,248 miles of IC lines or 81% of its total rail mileage. Piggyback trailers numbered 125, which were the newest 40-foot vans. Three IC switch engines power a piggyback train across Chicago in 1972. *Russ Porter*

ABOVE. The IC splits Kankakee about in the center; here #9096, a 1954-built GP-9, is in this Midwest industrial city to switch cars at the many factories and plants. The date is May, 1971. *Russ Porter*

IC #8967 GP-7 and another Geep in orange and white inhabit an IC roundhouse facility which has become rather inactive, if the weeds growing near the track are any indication. *Jerry Carson*

At Madison, Illinois the IC maintained connections with the Illinois Terminal, Litchfield & Madison and the Terminal RR Association of St. Louis. Here, #9500 sits at the yard office door. *Jerry Carson*

On a cold February day in late afternoon, a two-unit freight meanders down the tracks with several loads of heavy machinery. The IC usually generated more traffic than it received from other roads. In 1950, there were 500 connections with 150 other railroads; IC ran 56 regularly-scheduled daily dispatch trains to speed the freight. *Jerry Carson*

At Homewood, Illinois in 1969, IC #8952, a 1,500-hp unit, and BU-1, a home-built booster unit, combined for 80,000 pounds of tractive effort at 5.5 miles an hour. The booster had a 30-foot wheelbase and was 44'5" over pulling faces. *Owen Leander*

ABOVE. A lone IC diesel with train passes one of the numerous country roads on the system in October, 1977. *Russ Porter*
BELOW. The new split-rail diesel leads this trio. *Jerry Carson*

ABOVE. A bright IC Geep and train rumble into town. BELOW. Clinton, Illinois in the ICG era. *Both pictures, Russ Porter*

IC at first entered Iowa by leasing northern Iowa's pioneer railroad, then the Dubuque & Sioux City, in 1867; earlier in 1853, the Iowa legislature granted a charter to the Dubuque & Pacific to build from Dubuque westwardly on the best route toward the Pacific Ocean. Later, the Dubuque & Sioux City RR, heir to the D&P, was leased to the IC. By 1870, the IC operated 402 miles of Iowa trackage. Russ Porter caught these black Geeps in Iowa in July, 1963.

At East St. Louis, Illinois, #9302 sits and waits for assignment.
Jerry Carson

Running fast through the green fields and forests the IC serves nearly systemwide, #8022 and sisters haul a freight toward its destination over heavy rail. Between 1945 and 1950, the IC laid 1,458 miles of new rail, varying from 183 to 308 miles per year. Most of this was 112- and 115-lb rail. *Jerry Carson*

A three-unit freight rolls near Elgin, Illinois in 1967, the year the IC and Gulf, Mobile & Ohio made a merger announcement. The year 1967 also saw some very heavy snows in IC territory, which cost the IC revenue. The IC reorganized the passenger department in 1967 with the objective to promote the passenger services on trains the public liked, to develop fresh types of service and cut loss-producing services quickly. *Russ Porter*

A local makes the turn on the Gilman to Springfield line as a fast-moving IC passenger train makes the miles in the near background. Gilman was part of the IC's "racetrack" segment south of Chicago where trains were allowed speeds up to 90 mph. Given the heavy rail, flat prairie and tight schedules, IC trains pushed the miles back quickly on this portion of the railroad. *Russ Porter*

Several black Geeps and an orange and white Geep depict the differences between the schemes. The brighter colors gave the railroad an appealing visual image. *Jerry Carson*

A 1,750-hp GP-9 rebuilt to a 1,850 hp GP-10 heads up a caboose hop in December, 1969. *Jerry Carson*

Locomotives #3021-3029-3030 head up freight train #51 with a total of 9,000 hp. These GP-40s, passing through Homewood, Illinois in September of 1971, were built in 1966. *Jerry Carson*

Diesels on the Illinois Central

BU-1 was IC's slug converted in October of 1952 from SW1 #9017 at IC's own Paducah Shops. *Owen Leander*

HU-4 was one of six heater cars built at Chicago's Burnside Shop on refrigerator car frames. *Owen Leander*

HU-5 heater car contained two Clarkson steam generators. *Owen Leander*

Illinois Central switcher #13 was a 600 hp SW-1 built in 1946. *Jerry Carson*

The 1,200-hp SW-7 #200 was previously numbered #1200. *Jerry Carson*

A 1,200-hp SW-7 built in June, 1950. *Jerry Carson*

IC #436, 1,200-hp SW-9 in black and white livery. *Jerry Carson*

Originally a Peabody Coal RS-2, #703 was one of three such units. *Owen Leander*

EMC 1,000 hp NW-2 was built in December of 1939. *Jerry Carson*

In June, 1970 we see 1945-built 1,000 hp NW-2. *Owen Leander*

TR-A was one of two such 1,000 hp IC units, shown at Chicago. *Owen Leander*

IC #1208 1,200 hp SW-7 built in 1950 shown at Cicero, Ill. *Owen Leander*

A big, husky-looking Alco 3,600 hp C-636 at Paducah in 1969. *Richard Wallin*

IC's merger with the GM&O yielded #1133, an RS-1E Alco. Collection of Don Heimburger

A 1950-built SW-7 with 1,200 hp in 1966 at Cicero, Illinois. *Owen Leander*

Now gone from the IC, this 1,300 hp EMD SW-13 was rebuilt at Paducah in 1972. *Jerry Carson*

EMD SW-13 began as a 1,200 hp unit but was rebuilt to a 1,300 hp diesel. *Jerry Carson*

In Chicago, sharp looking #1401 was rebuilt in 1978 at Paducah to an SW-14. *Jerry Carson*

At Centralia, #1413 with squared off roof is a 1,300 hp EMD switcher; note lights over windows. *Jerry Carson*

Originally GM&O #800, now ICG F3-A #1610. *Jerry Carson*

Originally GM&O F7-A #811, then #812-A, and later IC #1615. *David Ingles, collection of Jerry Carson*

F3-A IC #1620 at Glenn Yard, Chicago, in 1975. *Bill Raia, collection of Don Heimburger*

"The American Eagle" was IC's bicentennial diesel. Shown at Fulton, Kentucky. *Jerry Carson*

#2272 was a former GM&O GP-30, built between 1962-3 by EMD. *Jerry Carson*

A former GM&O GP-35, #2503, delivered with Alco trucks. *Jerry Carson*

Another former GM&O GP-35, #2514 shown was built in 1964-1965. *Jerry Carson*

A 3,000-hp GP-40 #3008 built in 1966 offered lots of horsepower for IC freights. *Jerry Carson*

EMD-built GP-40 No. 3011 was one of 76 of these units purchased in the late '60s. *Owen Leander*

Russ Porter photographed orange and white GP-40 #3013 in September, 1971 at Chicago.

GP-40 #3014 is at Bastrop, Louisiana in 1982. *Jerry Carson*

Another GP-40 #3037 still in original black paint scheme. *Jerry Carson*

GE-built U33C, a 3,300 hp growler was one of 10 such IC diesels. *Jerry Carson*

IC #6015 was one of 13 SD-40As built in 1969 for the IC line. *Jerry Carson*

Former GM&O #6070 was an SD-40 built in 1966. *Jerry Carson*

Originally built in 1954 as a GP-9, this unit was rebuilt to a GP-10. *Jerry Carson*

IC was proud of its diesel rebuildings: #8052 was just out of the shops. *Collection of Don Heimburger*

Here's Geep #8052 again, having seen some years of service. Madison, Illinois, December 28, 1973. *Jerry Carson*

Just a month earlier in June of 1969, #8060 had been rebuilt to a GP-10. *Owen Leander*

Six months ago #8070 was a GP-9; now it's a GP-10 in June of 1970. *David Ingles, collection of Don Heimburger*

GP-10 #8107 was one of many IC diesels upgraded in 1969. *Jerry Carson*

IC #8193 was one of 107 locos rebuilt or upgraded in 1970. *Jerry Carson*

In a display near Central Station in September, 1972, #8279 GP-10 sits among other exhibits. *Jerry Carson*

In a combination of colors and diesel types sits IC #8906, a 1,500-hp GP-7. To the right is former GM&O F-3 #806-A, whose number hadn't been changed yet. *Jerry Carson*

Black Geep #9050 stands tall, after serving the IC since 1954; date is May, 1973. *Jerry Carson*

#9318 was one of 44 such 1,750-hp GP-9s delivered in 1957. *Owen Leander*

In June of 1968, several vestages of IC steam power days remained, and even in downtown Chicago as this old, black water tower attests. In front is Geep GP-9 #9332. *Owen Leander*

#9108 has been marked with a white "x" on its forehead. *Jerry Carson*

IC #9110 appears as if it has just passed beneath the St. Louis Gateway Arch. *Jerry Carson*

Three black Geeps are serviced in this now-long gone scene. *Jerry Carson*

Geep #9194, a GP-9, drifts through town with a local freight. *Jerry Carson*

IC #9206 built in 1957 is shown here in 1974. *Jerry Carson*

The green diamond held up well on Geep #9221. *Jerry Carson*

GP-9 has lost its IC lettering in the diamond in 1973. *Jerry Carson*

A newly repainted GP-9 #9360 looks good in September 1971. *Jerry Carson*

GP-18 #9402 contains 1,800 hp and was built in 1960. *Jerry Carson*

A low-nose EMD GP-18 #9424 helped give engine crews better visibility. *Jerry Carson*

A GP-28 low-nose with 1,800 hp that was built in 1964. *Jerry Carson*

The last numbered GP-28 originally delivered to the IC was #9440. *Jerry Carson*

A GP-38AC with 2,000 hp, #9504 teams up with GM&O #751 GP-38-2. *Jerry Carson*

IC #9510 was one of 20 GP-38ACs delivered in 1970. *Jerry Carson*

Two new GP-38ACs arrive on IC property. *Jerry Carson*

Passenger Trains

The IC Chicago coach yards south of Central Station on a cold day are busy as a transfer run headed by switchers at left parallel tracks of the elevated connecting St. Charles Air Line, not in picture. *Russ Porter*

IC #4037, a 2,400 hp E-9A diesel leads off a three-unit set of power for an IC train awaiting departure time at Chicago Central Station in 1963. *Owen Leander*

The streamlined *Green Diamond* was a sensation when it began service between Chicago and St. Louis in May of 1936; the green five-car train consisted of lightweight cars which were integral to one another. *Glass plate courtesy Rich Gajnak*

LEFT. Used as the cover of the 1959 Illinois Central Annual Report, this scene at the Champaign, Illinois depot shows passengers boarding the *Panama Limited* during the 1959-60 winter season. The *Panama Limited* and the *City of Miami* leased dome cars for the winter from the Pullman Company, one on the *Panama* and two on the *City*. *Collection of Don Heimburger*

IC streamliner cuts through old concrete coal bunker in 1960 which straddle the main line. *Clayton Tanner*

TOP. It's May of 1971, and Amtrak has taken over most of the nation's passenger trains, including this IC passenger train parked momentarily at Kankakee on a balmy spring evening. *Russ Porter*

Two E-6s power the last run of the *Governor's Special* on April 30, 1971 at Springfield, Illinois. *Richard Wallin*

In March of 1969, IC #4033, an E-8 with 2,250 hp powered by four EMD D27 traction motors, leads a passenger run out of the yards south of Chicago's Central Station. *Owen Leander*

BELOW. On this March, 1967 day near Elgin, Illinois, IC's *Land O'Corn* consists of just three passenger cars, one of which is a baggage. The piggyback Flexi-Vans carry mail; the Chicago to Waterloo, Iowa train was discontinued later that year. *Russ Porter*

ABOVE. Main Line of Mid-America from the cab of a passenger diesel. *Jerry Carson*

ABOVE. The *Panama Limited* makes its presence felt as the engineer cuts the engines as Train #5 approaches the Wabash diamond at Tolono, Illinois, eight miles south of Champaign on a warm summer evening in 1967. The IC agent-operator greets the train with a friendly wave and a watchful eye. As the locomotives move over the crossing, the train accelerates in a defeaning roar, and the noise of the Pullman cars being led at 90 miles an hour trails off gradually into the humid Illinois prairie air. *Clayton Tanner*

The eastbound *Land O' Corn*, which left Waterloo, Iowa at 6:45 a.m. will arrive, barring difficulties, in Chicago at 12:15. *Russ Porter*.

BELOW. May of 1968 sees a coach train with piggyback cars tacked to the rear. *Don Heimburger collection*

Locomotive #4035 leads a long, sleek IC streamliner in November of 1957. *Philip Weibler*

ABOVE. IC's Central Station train shed was always a busy place with trains ready to depart and others being broken up by switchers after arrival. In August of 1963, #4026 and sister are at the headend of one of IC's trains. In 1963, IC operated nine business cars and 56 streamlined Pullman cars. *Owen Leander*

The *City of New Orleans*, trains 1 and 2, began service with lightweight equipment the year this photo was taken, in 1947. Note porters standing at car doors while train stands in Effingham, Illinois station. *Photo by Clayton Tanner, courtesy Dick Stair*

Split-rail IC #4028 leads the charge through Kankakee in May of 1971 with the *City of New Orleans* in tow; the railroad's new Woodcrest Shops were completed north of here adjacent to Markham Yard in 1971. *Russ Porter*

BELOW. IC passenger trains are holding on a siding at Gilman, Illinois in May of 1971, now being operated by the IC under contract with the National RR Passenger Corp. *Russ Porter*

ABOVE. E-7s pull the *Green Diamond*, a Chicago-St. Louis train first introduced on May 17, 1936 and later a Chicago-Springfield train renamed the *Governor's Special* in 1968. It's shown here in 1959 at Springfield with No. 4009 and a six-car consist. *Dick Wallin*

IC's #4016 sits on Chicago lakefront facilities awaiting servicing and the next run in 1965. Passenger revenues were up in 1965 to $14.1 million, a 5% increase from the year before. *Brad Smith*

ABOVE. A split-rail passenger diesel will be on its way again soon after a few minutes of servicing on one of its runs. *Jerry Carson*

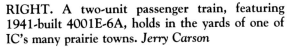

RIGHT. A two-unit passenger train, featuring 1941-built 4001E-6A, holds in the yards of one of IC's many prairie towns. *Jerry Carson*

A two-diesel-unit four-car orange and chocolate brown streamliner makes a station stop at Kanka-kee in May of 1971, the month and year Amtrak took over nationwide passenger service. The Chicago to Champaign route was heavily traveled by University of Illinois students, since thousands of Urbana campus students lived in the Chicago area. *Russ Porter*

A very long *City of New Orleans* stops at Kankakee in August of 1967 with three diesel units. The big news on the line in 1967 was the IC and GM&O merger. *Dick Wallin collection*

Eighty-one miles south of the Chicago River sits Gilman, Illinois where the Toledo, Peoria & Western crosses the main line of the IC. From Gilman, the line cuts southwesterly to Clinton. In June of 1971, the *City of New Orleans* barrels southbound through Gilman. *Russ Porter*

Passenger Diesels

One of very few 2,000 hp E-6s sits at Chicago in February of 1970, 29 years after she was built. Originally, Nos. 4001-4004 were lettered "Panama Limited." The long, sleek nose is of the Art Deco styling in vogue at the time. *Owen Leander*

Three years prior to when the photo above was taken, the #4001 featured the green diamond logo on the nose, a trademark of the Illinois Central for many years. *Owen Leander*

E-6 #4003 singlehandedly handles Train #302 from Central Station over the IC and the New York Central to Cincinnati, Ohio in 1967. *Owen Leander*

Looking sharp in Chicago in 1967 is #4004, another 1941 EMD locomotive project. *Owen Leander*

LEFT. In spring of 1970 #4003 sits in front of a roundhouse in Chicago. *Collection of Don Heimburger*

With IC's passenger department completely reorganized in 1967, a 1946-built E-7 #4009 looks pristine and ready to sell passenger service to the public. *Owen Leander*

A day after July 4 in 1965, #4012 E-7 awaits assignment hauling more of the passengers that increased passenger revenues that year by five per cent. *Owen Leander*

An ABA combination with the split-rail design is positioned for a fast retreat from Central Station once the highball is given. *Owen Leander*

A 1951-built EMD E-8 is coupled to a leased Denver & Rio Grande Western unit on July 12, 1969 at Chicago. When this photo was taken, oatmeal in the diner was $.60, broiled smoked ham with eggs was $1.75, and wheat cakes with maple syrup was $1.40. *Owen Leander*

#4022 EMD E-8 with green diamond logo in 1965. *Owen Leander*

#4022 with split-rail logo, larger letters on the sides and brown chocolate paint around the nose. *Jerry Carson*

A 1954 E-9 #4035 shown in 1967. *Jerry Carson*

An EMD E-9 #4039. *Jerry Carson*

#4042 E-9 sees a crew change. *Jerry Carson*

#4043 E-9 with its boss, William B. Johnson, president, during ad campaign in downtown Chicago. *Collection of Don Heimburger*

B units

#4105 E-8 B unit built in 1952. *Owen Leander*

#4106 E-9 B unit built in 1956. *Owen Leander*

Central of Georgia

A blue/orange/black/grey/yellow E unit in 1954 teams with an IC diesel in a pooling arrangement to transport passengers to Florida destinations such as Jacksonville, Tampa and Naples. Photo was taken from the IC tower at Champaign in 1954. *Dick Stair*

Shiny Central of Georgia diesel #812 dressed up in Illinois Central colors and a CofG green diamond logo sits in Chicago on July 1, 1967. *Owen Leander*

BELOW. Central of Georgia coach #506 is hard to distinguish from IC-painted equipment. Photo was taken October 26, 1968 in Chicago. *Owen Leander*

RIGHT. Central of Georgia single A unit diesel #812 was used on the four-car *Green Diamond* at Springfield, Illinois in June of 1968. *Dick Wallin*

CofG #811 in IC paint leads a three unit diesel combination on June 13, 1970 south out of Chicago's Central Station. *Owen Leander*

Passenger Cars

The #160 postal-mail storage/RPO was one of only several such cars in 1969 on the IC; they were 85 feet long. *Owen Leander*

This is #568, a 64-foot-long storage and express car with an arched roof. *Owen Leander*

Arch roof REA baggage-magazine loading car #760 is lined out in summer of 1968, ready for scrapping. *Owen Leander*

Baggage car #1839 is gleaming bright at Kankakee in May of 1971. *Russ Porter*

Baggage-coach #1850 sat 36 patrons and contained 29 feet of baggage storage space. *Owen Leander*

Virtually windowless #1906 baggage-dormitory slept crew members in relative comfort. *Owen Leander*

Coach #2622 had a capacity of 56 and was 85 feet in length. *Owen Leander*

Coach #2639 was one of 27 such cars the IC owned in spring of 1970. *Owen Leander*

Heavyweight coach #2716 sat 64 passengers over its long six-axle trucks. *Owen Leander*

Coach-dormitory car #2732 had a dormitory capacity of 6, and 46 seat passenger capacity. *Owen Leander*

Coach #2685 sat 48 with its 79 foot length on six-wheel trucks. *Owen Leander*

Long, sleek coach #2804 was 81 feet long; car had electro-mechanical air conditioning. *Owen Leander*

Coach #2900 sat 76 passengers in its 71 feet of interior space. *Owen Leander*

Food-bar-coach #3345 has a capacity of 44 in coach and eight in the food section. *Owen Leander*

Split-rail design #3513 sleeper is the *Centralia* with 10 roomettes and six double bedrooms. *Owen Leander*

Thirty-two-seat parlor car #3351 ran on the *Panama Limited* between Jackson and New Orleans. *Owen Leander*

Diner #4102 *Vieux Carre* ran in *Panama Limited* trains until the early 1950s. *Owen Leander*

Diner-lounge #4110 has a capacity of 48 as a full diner or 32 as a diner-lounge. *Owen Leander*

Diner #4175 sat 56 patrons; there was also a #4175A which was a kitchen-dormitory car. *Owen Leander*

City trains dome-coach car #2202 was built in 1948, acquired from the Missouri Pacific in 1967. *Owen Leander*

Pullman-Standard-built 1952 dome-coach #2211 seats 52 on lower level, 24 in dome. *Owen Leander*

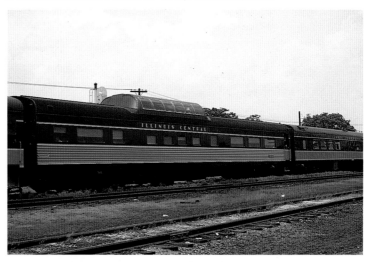

Fluted side dome-coach was one of six the IC purchased to enliven its passenger service prior to Amtrak. *Jerry Carson*

Ten roomette/six double bedroom Pullman #3517 was the *Clifton*. It slept 22. *Owen Leander*

IC #3504 was the *Bradley*, an 11 double bedroom car that slept 22. *Owen Leander*

The beautiful *Baton Rouge* Pullman, #3500, was an 85-foot-long revenue-maker for the IC. Photo was taken in 1968. *Owen Leander*

The *Central City* was Pullman car #3527 and contained 10 roomettes and 6 double bedrooms. *Owen Leander*

The 85-foot Pullman *Chicagoland* #3540 photographed in Windy City in October of 1969. *Owen Leander*

The Pullman *Galena* contained 4 double bedrooms, 4 compartments and 2 drawing rooms. *Owen Leander*

Pullman *Magnolia State* featured 6 sections, 6 roomettes and 4 double bedrooms. *Owen Leander*

Pullman *Banana Road* slept 26 over roller bearing trucks; lightweight was 137,700 lbs. *Owen Leander*

Pullman *Belleville* contained 11 double bedrooms, sleeping 22. *Owen Leander*

Pullman *Timberland* was photographed in Chicago on March 3, 1968. *Owen Leander*

Nearly all of IC's business cars were heavyweights; this one is traveling through Kankakee. *Russ Porter*

Office car-observation #9 is attached to an outgoing southbound passenger train from Central Station in Chicago. *Owen Leander*

Office car #6 rests between trips in Chicago's passenger coach yard. The 83' 3" heavyweight observation was the heaviest office car on the IC in June of 1970 when this photo was taken. It contained a vapor hot water heater and Waukesha air conditioning. *Owen Leander*

A *Panama Limited* lightweight observation with green diamond logo and end rear light burning warmly, brings up another edition of this famous train on a cold, snowy day. In May of 1942, lightweight *Panama* equipment went into service. *Jerry Carson*

Flatend observation-bar-lounge #3314 had a capacity of 47; radio antenna adorns its roof. With modified observation end, the car was suitable for midtrain use. *Owen Leander*

BELOW. Observation-bar-lounge #3305 was an 81-foot car used on the *City of New Orleans*. Photo was taken June 29, 1969. *Owen Leander*

Old Electric Equipment

ABOVE. The 1100-series electric suburban cars were 72'8" in length over buffers (60' inside passenger compartment) and sat 84 commuters. The system carried 107,000 passengers every day on 335 trains. IC suburban service had 54 stations, three of which served Chicago's Loop; seven interlocking plants that controlled movement; 140 motor cars and a like amount of trailers. Service began in July of 1856, and was the first commuter service west of Philadelphia. *Brad Smith*

LEFT. IC suburban service operated three types of trains—locals, express and specials, maintaining on-time performance of between 95 and 98 percent. The equipment was operated in units of one motor car and one trailer, semi-permanently coupled. The dark green cars with rattan seats were not fancy, only fast. *Brad Smith*

NEXT PAGE, TOP. Traveling in multiples as much as 10, IC's Pullman-built electric cars ran over 42.33 miles of electrified line. *Charles Zeiler* BOTTOM. A typical scene in 1969 at 12th Street Station on the suburban service; the station also served IC employees who worked at Central Station. The line had two branches, the South Chicago branch and the Blue Island branch. *Russ Porter*

New Electric Equipment

Rushing past old electric equipment in the adjacent yard, new highliner cars built in 1971 gave the commuter service a new image and a top speed of 75 mph. *Russ Porter*

This spring, 1974 photo shows one of the new 85-foot bi-level 152-patron cars at a station platform. Passengers board by entering a large double door at the center of the car; cars operate on 1,500 volt d.c. power from overhead wires. *Jerry Carson*

A grant of $25.2 million was put towards 130 of the new cars. Eleven Chicago suburbs participated in the mass transit district. *Jerry Carson*

Work Equipment

ICX101 was an Industrial Works 150-ton wrecking crane stationed at Carbondale, Illinois. It covered the St. Louis Division south and west of DuQuoin and north of Ballard and Reevesville. *Jerry Carson*

IC X115 Orton crane has been repainted in IC orange and black with the split-rail logo. *Jerry Carson*

In 1963, the IC operated 41 different wrecking and locomotive cranes to service the property, from manufacturers such as Bucyrus, Orton, Shaw, Browning, Brownhoist and others. *Jerry Carson*

ICG #100405 with orange cab, black frame and silver-painted hook ends was located at Carbondale in the fall of 1982, along with other work cars. *Jerry Carson*

Wrecking crane #100412 wears the orange paint of the ICG in 1983 at Wamac, Illinois. *Jerry Carson*

Diesel sand car #X689 and sister were part of a fleet of as many as 50 the IC operated on the system. *Jerry Carson*

The IC favored gondolas converted to snowplows; here #X8034 and sister hides next to the roundhouse in 1981. Twenty years earlier the IC operated 26 of these. *Jerry Carson*

Cabooses

Between 1948 and 1954, the IC rebuilt a series of 30-foot terminal wood cabooses in their shops for themselves and the Chicago & Illinois Western. The series included 8000 to 8115. This one is on the Springfield Division in June of 1954. *Jerry Carson*

At Evansville, Indiana in 1954, is steel underframe cupola caboose #9193. In 1963 the IC owned 61 such cars. *Jerry Carson*

In 1970, the IC built 50 shock-control cushion underframe 30-foot steel cabooses such as #9464; the cars utilized Barber swing motion trucks. *Jerry Carson*

The ICG purchased these Eastern-type 24-foot steel cabooses from the Pennsylvania Railroad in 1974. Constructed in 1951, the Pennsy built them in their shops. The cars had a fuel oil capacity of 35 gallons and 30 gallons of water. This car is at Council Bluffs, Iowa. *Jerry Carson*

Old caboose #199755 is repainted in the striking orange and black of the ICG in April of 1974. The crew added a touch of home with window curtains. *Jerry Carson*

ICG steel caboose #199817 rolls at the end of a train in the St. Louis area in 1975. A TRRA diesel switcher rumbles past on the overhead bridge. *Jerry Carson*

Around the Railroad

Index

annual report
for the year ended December 31, 1954

ILLINOIS CENTRAL RAILROAD
Main Line of Mid-America